PRENTICE HALL MATHEMATICS

COURSES 1–3
PRE-ALGEBRA

Algebra
Readiness
Tests

PEARSON

Prentice
Hall

Boston, Massachusetts
Upper Saddle River, New Jersey

ISBN 0-13-201390-8

7 8 9 10 V004 12 11 10

Contents

Reviewers of Algebra Readiness Tests

Teachers from the following locations reviewed tests in this book and provided input on content and format. Prentice Hall gratefully acknowledges their contribution.

Alpharetta, Georgia
Chambler, Georgia
Snellville, Georgia
Arlington Heights, Illinois
Des Plaines, Illinois
Elmhurst, Illinois
Glenview, Illinois
Mt. Prospect, Illinois
Naperville, Illinois
Woodstock, Illinois
Lenexa, Kansas
Overland Park, Kansas
Prairie Village, Kansas
North East, Maryland
Blue Springs, Missouri
Liberty, Missouri
Lee's Summit, Missouri
Fair Lawn, New Jersey
Ridgefield, New Jersey
Rochelle Park, New Jersey
Secaucus, New Jersey
Henderson, Nevada
Las Vegas, Nevada
Cincinnati, Ohio
Philadelphia, Pennsylvania

Introduction

The tests in this book are designed as a tool to help teachers decide whether students are ready to move on to a full Algebra course. Keep in mind, this is only one tool to use. Combine it with the many other indicators you already use, such as:

◆ performance in other tests during the school year
◆ homework and other assessment tools, such as projects and journals
◆ nationally-normed ability and aptitude tests
◆ school district tests
◆ school attendance and attitude
◆ organizational skills
◆ study habits

Here's how to use Algebra Readiness Tests:

During the school year	1. Assess students' grasp of the basic skills they need to move on to Algebra.
	2. Remediate as the school year progresses.
At the end of the school year	3. Assess students' algebra concept-readiness.
	4. Evaluate whether students are ready to move on to a full Algebra course.

1. *Assess students' grasp of the basic skills they need to move on to Algebra.*

Use a *Basic Skills Test* to assess your students' grasp of the basic skills associated with Algebra readiness:

1. Decimal Operations
2. Factors and Prime Numbers
3. Fraction Operations
4. Exponent Awareness
5. Proportional Reasoning
6. Percents
7. Finding Perimeter, Area, and Volume
8. Integer Awareness
9. Integer Operations
10. Translating Words to Mathematical Expressions
11. Solving One-Step Equations

The test comes in four equivalent forms, A, B, C, and D. Questions are in multiple-choice format for easy grading.

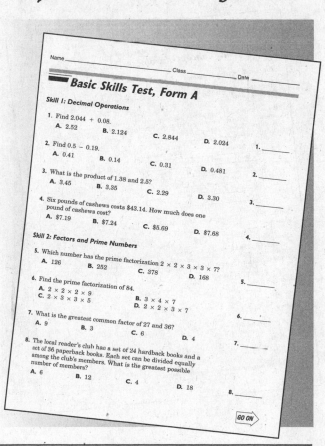

Name _____ Class _____ Date _____

Basic Skills Test, Form A

Skill 1: Decimal Operations

1. Find 2.044 + 0.08.
   A. 2.52 B. 2.124 C. 2.844 D. 2.024 1. _____

2. Find 0.5 − 0.19.
   A. 0.41 B. 0.14 C. 0.31 D. 0.481 2. _____

3. What is the product of 1.38 and 2.5?
   A. 3.45 B. 3.35 C. 2.29 D. 3.30 3. _____

4. Six pounds of cashews costs $43.14. How much does one pound of cashews cost?
   A. $7.19 B. $7.24 C. $5.69 D. $7.68 4. _____

Skill 2: Factors and Prime Numbers

5. Which number has the prime factorization 2 × 2 × 3 × 3 × 7?
   A. 126 B. 252 C. 378 D. 168 5. _____

6. Find the prime factorization of 84.
   A. 2 × 2 × 2 × 9 B. 3 × 4 × 7
   C. 2 × 3 × 3 × 5 D. 2 × 2 × 3 × 7 6. _____

7. What is the greatest common factor of 27 and 36?
   A. 9 B. 3 C. 6 D. 4 7. _____

8. The local reader's club has a set of 24 hardback books and a set of 36 paperback books. Each set can be divided equally among the club's members. What is the greatest possible number of members?
   A. 6 B. 12 C. 4 D. 18 8. _____

GO ON →

2. Remediate as the school year progress.

After you administer a Basic Skills Test during the school year, use the *Student Progress Chart* for follow-up.

◆ Determine where students need more skills work.
◆ Prescribe remediation.
◆ Share the chart with students as well as parents or guardians.

You can set the criteria, determine whether a skill has been demonstrated, and choose the follow-up you think appropriate.

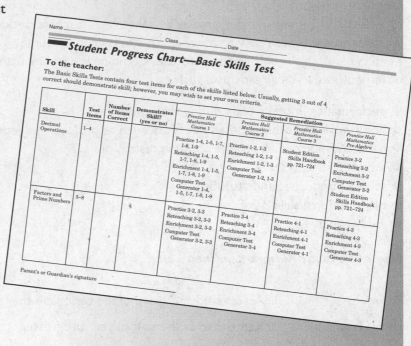

Name _____
Class _____ Date _____

Student Progress Chart—Basic Skills Test

To the teacher:
The Basic Skills Tests contain four test items for each of the skills listed below. Usually, getting 3 out of 4 correct should demonstrate skill; however, you may wish to set your own criteria.

Skill	Test Items	Number of Items Correct	Demonstrates Skill? (yes or no)	Suggested Remediation			
				Prentice Hall Mathematics Course 1	*Prentice Hall Mathematics Course 2*	*Prentice Hall Mathematics Course 3*	*Prentice Hall Mathematics Pre-Algebra*
Decimal Operations	1–4			Practice 1-4, 1-5, 1-7, 1-8, 1-9 Reteaching 1-4, 1-5, 1-7, 1-8, 1-9 Enrichment 1-4, 1-5, 1-7, 1-8, 1-9 Computer Test Generator 1-4, 1-5, 1-7, 1-8, 1-9	Practice 1-2, 1-3 Reteaching 1-2, 1-3 Enrichment 1-2, 1-3 Computer Test Generator 1-2, 1-3	Student Edition Skills Handbook pp. 721–724	Practice 3-2 Reteaching 3-2 Enrichment 3-2 Computer Test Generator 3-2 Student Edition Skills Handbook pp. 721–724
Factors and Prime Numbers	5–8			Practice 3-2, 3-3 Reteaching 3-2, 3-3 Enrichment 3-2, 3-3 Computer Test Generator 3-2, 3-3	Practice 3-4 Reteaching 3-4 Enrichment 3-4 Computer Test Generator 3-4	Practice 4-1 Reteaching 4-1 Enrichment 4-1 Computer Test Generator 4-1	Practice 4-3 Reteaching 4-3 Enrichment 4-3 Computer Test Generator 4-3

Parent's or Guardian's signature _____

3. Assess students' readiness.

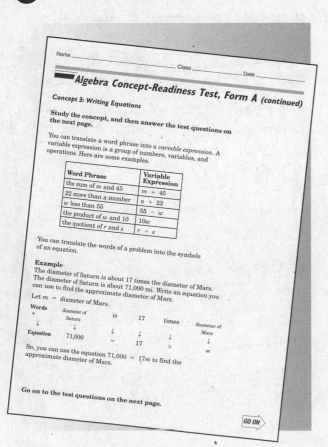

Name _____
Class _____ Date _____

Algebra Concept-Readiness Test, Form A (continued)

Concept 3: Writing Equations

Study the concept, and then answer the test questions on the next page.

You can translate a word phrase into a *variable expression*. A variable expression is a group of numbers, variables, and operations. Here are some examples.

Word Phrase	Variable Expression
the sum of m and 45	$m + 45$
22 more than a number	$n + 22$
w less than 55	$55 - w$
the product of w and 10	$10w$
the quotient of r and s	$r \div s$

You can translate the words of a problem into the symbols of an equation.

Example
The diameter of Saturn is about 17 times the diameter of Mars. The diameter of Saturn is about 71,000 mi. Write an equation you can use to find the approximate diameter of Mars.
Let m = diameter of Mars.

Words: diameter of Saturn is 17 times diameter of Mars
Equation: $71{,}000 = 17 \times m$

So, you can use the equation $71{,}000 = 17m$ to find the approximate diameter of Mars.

Go on to the test questions on the next page.

GO ON

At the end of the school year, use both a Basic Skills Test and an *Algebra Concept-Readiness Test*. The Concept-Readiness Test helps you assess student readiness for acquiring algebra skills. The test comes in two equivalent forms, A and B, and it includes these concepts:

1. The Distributive Property
2. Roots and Powers
3. Writing Equations
4. Solving Equations Using the Properties of Equality
5. Graphing

For each concept, students study a page of instruction...

Each part of an Algebra Concept-Readiness Test begins with a short, simple explanation of an algebra concept. Examples show students how to apply each concept.

*. . . then complete a page
of exercises*

After students study an algebra concept, they try it for themselves. Each concept explanation is followed by a page of exercises.

Each test has 30 exercises in multiple-choice format for easy grading.

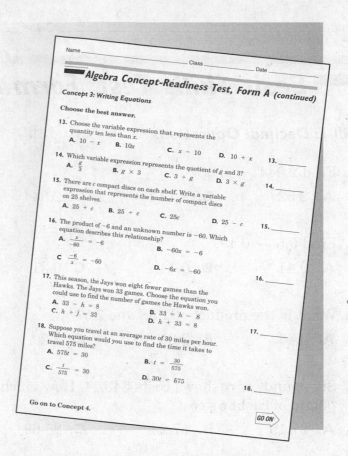

Name _____ Class _____ Date _____

Algebra Concept-Readiness Test, Form A (continued)

Concept 3: Writing Equations

Choose the best answer.

13. Choose the variable expression that represents the quantity ten less than x.
 A. $10 - x$ B. $10x$ C. $x - 10$ D. $10 + x$ 13. _____

14. Which variable expression represents the quotient of g and 3?
 A. $\frac{g}{3}$ B. $g \times 3$ C. $3 \div g$ D. $3 \times g$ 14. _____

15. There are c compact discs on each shelf. Write a variable expression that represents the number of compact discs on 25 shelves.
 A. $25 + c$ B. $25 \div c$ C. $25c$ D. $25 - c$ 15. _____

16. The product of -6 and an unknown number is -60. Which equation describes this relationship?
 A. $\frac{x}{-60} = -6$
 B. $-60x = -6$
 C. $\frac{-6}{x} = -60$
 D. $-6x = -60$ 16. _____

17. This season, the Jays won eight fewer games than the Hawks. The Jays won 33 games. Choose the equation you could use to find the number of games the Hawks won.
 A. $33 - h = 8$ B. $33 = h - 8$
 C. $h + j = 33$ D. $h + 33 = 8$ 17. _____

18. Suppose you travel at an average rate of 30 miles per hour. Which equation would you use to find the time it takes to travel 575 miles?
 A. $575t = 30$
 B. $t = \frac{30}{575}$
 C. $\frac{t}{575} = 30$
 D. $30t = 575$ 18. _____

Go on to Concept 4.

GO ON →

4. *Evaluate whether students are ready to move on to a full Algebra course.*

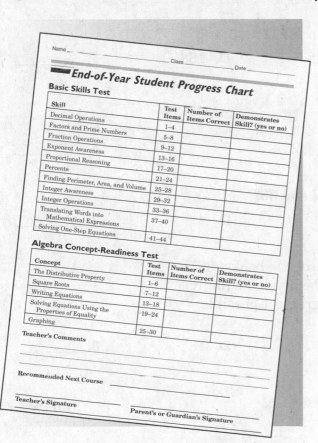

Name _____ Class _____ Date _____

End-of-Year Student Progress Chart

Basic Skills Test

Skill	Test Items	Number of Items Correct	Demonstrates Skill? (yes or no)
Decimal Operations	1–4		
Factors and Prime Numbers	5–8		
Fraction Operations	9–12		
Exponent Awareness	13–16		
Proportional Reasoning	17–20		
Percents	21–24		
Finding Perimeter, Area, and Volume	25–28		
Integer Awareness	29–32		
Integer Operations	33–36		
Translating Words into Mathematical Expressions	37–40		
Solving One-Step Equations	41–44		

Algebra Concept-Readiness Test

Concept	Test Items	Number of Items Correct	Demonstrates Skill? (yes or no)
The Distributive Property	1–6		
Square Roots	7–12		
Writing Equations	13–18		
Solving Equations Using the Properties of Equality	19–24		
Graphing	25–30		

Teacher's Comments

_____
_____

Recommended Next Course _____

Teacher's Signature _____

Parent's or Guardian's Signature _____

At the end of the school year, administer a Basic Skills Test and an Algebra Concept-Readiness Test. Not all students are ready for Algebra at the same time, so *Algebra Readiness Tests* includes multiple copies of parallel tests that can be administered two years in a row—for students who are not ready to move into Algebra during the first year tested.

You can use the tests and the *End-of-Year Student Progress Chart* to help create an Algebra-readiness profile for each student.

The End-of-Year Student Progress Chart can be shared with students as well as parents or guardians. *Algebra Readiness Tests* also includes sample letters you can send home to students' families, explaining the purpose of the tests.

Basic Skills Test, Form A

Skill 1: Decimal Operations

1. Find 2.044 + 0.08.
   A. 2.52　　　　**B.** 2.124　　　　**C.** 2.844　　　　**D.** 2.024　　　　1. _____

2. Find 0.5 − 0.19.
   A. 0.41　　　　**B.** 0.14　　　　**C.** 0.31　　　　**D.** 0.481　　　　2. _____

3. What is the product of 1.38 and 2.5?
   A. 3.45　　　　**B.** 3.35　　　　**C.** 2.29　　　　**D.** 3.30　　　　3. _____

4. Six pounds of cashews costs $43.14. How much does one pound of cashews cost?
   A. $7.19　　　　**B.** $7.24　　　　**C.** $5.69　　　　**D.** $7.68　　　　4. _____

Skill 2: Factors and Prime Numbers

5. Which number has the prime factorization $2 \times 2 \times 3 \times 3 \times 7$?
   A. 126　　　　**B.** 252　　　　**C.** 378　　　　**D.** 168　　　　5. _____

6. Find the prime factorization of 84.
   A. $2 \times 2 \times 2 \times 9$　　　　　　**B.** $3 \times 4 \times 7$
   C. $2 \times 3 \times 3 \times 5$　　　　　　**D.** $2 \times 2 \times 3 \times 7$　　　　6. _____

7. What is the greatest common factor of 27 and 36?
   A. 9　　　　**B.** 3　　　　**C.** 6　　　　**D.** 4　　　　7. _____

8. The local reader's club has a set of 24 hardback books and a set of 36 paperback books. Each set can be divided equally among the club's members. What is the greatest possible number of members?
   A. 6　　　　**B.** 12　　　　**C.** 4　　　　**D.** 18　　　　8. _____

GO ON →

Basic Skills Test, Form A (continued)

Skill 3: Fraction Operations

9. Find $\frac{3}{8} + \frac{5}{6}$.

   A. $1\frac{7}{8}$ **B.** $1\frac{1}{3}$ **C.** $1\frac{5}{24}$ **D.** $1\frac{5}{12}$ 9._____

10. Find $5\frac{3}{4} - 2\frac{3}{8}$.

    A. $3\frac{3}{4}$ **B.** $2\frac{5}{8}$ **C.** $3\frac{1}{2}$ **D.** $3\frac{3}{8}$ 10._____

11. What is the product of $\frac{3}{4}$ and $3\frac{1}{5}$?

    A. $2\frac{1}{5}$ **B.** $3\frac{3}{20}$ **C.** $2\frac{1}{4}$ **D.** $2\frac{2}{5}$ 11._____

12. Find $\frac{3}{10} \div \frac{4}{5}$.

    A. $\frac{3}{8}$ **B.** $\frac{6}{25}$ **C.** $\frac{2}{5}$ **D.** $\frac{1}{2}$ 12._____

Skill 4: Exponent Awareness

13. Simplify the expression $(6 - 3)^2$.

    A. 3   **B.** 0   **C.** 9   **D.** -3 13._____

14. Write the expression $0.2 \times 0.2 \times 0.2 \times 0.2 \times 0.2$ using exponents.

    A. $5^{0.2}$ **B.** 0.2^4 **C.** 0.2^5 **D.** $10^{0.2}$ 14._____

15. Simplify the expression $(-2)^4$.

    A. -16 **B.** 64   **C.** -64 **D.** 16   15._____

16. Which expression represents the volume of a cube whose edge length is 60 units?

    A. 60^3 **B.** $3(60)$ **C.** 3^{60} **D.** 6^{10} 16._____

GO ON ⟹

Basic Skills Test, Form A (continued)

Skill 5: Proportional Reasoning

17. Which ratio is *not* equivalent to the others?

   A. $3 : 5$ **B.** $6 : 10$ **C.** $9 : 15$ **D.** $4 : 7$ **17.** _____

18. What is the missing term in the proportion $\frac{y}{16} = \frac{18}{24}$?

   A. 12   **B.** 40   **C.** 9   **D.** 10   **18.** _____

19. Below are two similar figures. Find x.

   A. 10
   B. 40
   C. 50
   D. 60   **19.** _____

20. A map has a scale of 1 cm : 100 km. How many centimeters on the map represents 250 km?

   A. 0.4 cm   **B.** 25 cm   **C.** 2.5 cm   **D.** 4 cm   **20.** _____

Skill 6: Percents

21. Convert $\frac{1}{6}$ to percent. Round to the nearest tenth.

   A. 1.7%   **B.** 6%   **C.** 16.7%   **D.** 60%   **21.** _____

22. Which group does *not* consist of equivalent numbers?

   A. $\frac{8}{20}$, 0.4, 40%   **B.** $\frac{35}{10}$, 3.5, 350%

   C. $\frac{6}{12}$, 0.5, 50%   **D.** $\frac{5}{8}$, 0.7, 70%   **22.** _____

23. Suppose the sales tax rate is 6%. How much sales tax would be charged for an item priced at $60.00?

   A. $10.00   **B.** $3.60   **C.** $1.00   **D.** $.36   **23.** _____

24. 60 is 30% of what number?

   A. 200   **B.** 18   **C.** 180   **D.** 20   **24.** _____

GO ON →

Basic Skills Test, Form A (continued)

Skill 7: Finding Perimeter, Area, and Volume

25. Find the perimeter and area of a rectangle 4 in. wide and 6 in. long.
   A. 20 in. and 24 in.^{2} **B.** 10 in. and 24 in.^{2}
   C. 20 in. and 12 in.^{2} **D.** 10 in. and 12 in.^{2} 25. _____

26. What is the area of the triangle?
   A. 108 m^2
   B. 90 m^2
   C. 54 m^2
   D. 36 m^2 26. _____

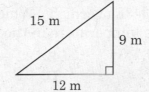

15 m

9 m

12 m

27. The formula for the area of a circle is πr^2. Find the diameter of a circle whose area is 314 cm^2.
   A. 10 cm   **B.** 100 cm   **C.** 200 cm   **D.** 20 cm   27. _____

28. What is the volume of a rectangular prism with length 9 ft, width 5 ft, and height 3 ft?
   A. 135 ft^3 **B.** 125 ft^3 **C.** 45 ft^3 **D.** 17 ft^3 28. _____

Skill 8: Integer Awareness

29. Choose the true statement.
   A. –3 < 3   **B.** –5 > 0   **C.** –7 > –6   **D.** 1 < –2   29. _____

30. The temperature on Mars ranges from –68°F during the day to –176°F at night. Which temperature is *not* likely to be measured on Mars?
   A. –100°F   **B.** 0°F   **C.** –76°F   **D.** –150°F   30. _____

31. Order the integers 0, –12, 18, 2, 15, and –1 from least to greatest.
   A. 0, –1, 2, –12, 15, 18   **B.** –1, –12, 0, 2, 15, 18
   C. –12, –1, 0, 2, 15, 18   **D.** 18, 15, 2, 0, –1, –12   31. _____

32. Which expression is *not* equivalent to the opposite of +9?
   A. –9   **B.** –|9| **C.** –|–9| **D.** |–9| 32. _____

Basic Skills Test, Form A (continued)

Skill 9: Integer Operations

33. Find the value of the expression $6 - 12 + (-6)$.

    A. 0   **B.** -12 **C.** 12   **D.** 6   **33.** _____

34. One night the temperature outside was 22°F . The temperature dropped 31°F overnight. Which expression can you use to find the temperature in the morning?

    A. $-31 + (-22)$ **B.** $22 - (-31)$

    C. $22 + (-31)$ **D.** $31 + (-22)$ **34.** _____

35. What is the product of -3 and -80?

    A. 240   **B.** -280 **C.** -240 **D.** 280   **35.** _____

36. Find $125 \div (-25)$.

    A. 100   **B.** 5   **C.** -25 **D.** -5 **36.** _____

Skill 10: Translating Words into Mathematical Expressions

37. Which variable expression corresponds to "10 less than a number"?

    A. $x \div 10$ **B.** $10 - x$ **C.** $x + 10$ **D.** $x - 10$ **37.** _____

38. Which word phrase could correspond to the variable expression $\frac{n}{15}$?

    A. 15 divided by a number   **B.** a number divided by 15

    C. 15 times a number   **D.** a number decreased by 15   **38.** _____

39. Write a variable expression that corresponds to "the product of 6 and t."

    A. $6 - t$ **B.** $6 + t$ **C.** $6t$ **D.** $6 \div t$ **39.** _____

40. A car travels m miles per hour. Which variable expression represents the number of miles traveled in 8 hours?

    A. $\frac{m}{8}$ **B.** $m - 8$ **C.** $8m$ **D.** $8 + m$ **40.** _____

GO ON →

Basic Skills Test, Form A (continued)

Skill 11: Solving One-Step Equations

41. Solve $x - 3 = -3$.

    A. 0   **B.** 3   **C.** -3 **D.** 6   **41.** _____

42. Solve $n + 1 = -4$.

    A. -3 **B.** -5 **C.** 5   **D.** 3   **42.** _____

43. Solve $56 = -8t$.

    A. 7   **B.** -8 **C.** 8   **D.** -7 **43.** _____

44. Solve $\dfrac{y}{-4} = -12$.

    A. 3   **B.** 48   **C.** -48 **D.** -3 **44.** _____

STOP

Basic Skills Test, Form B

Skill 1: Decimal Operations

1. Find $2.066 + 0.08$.

   A. 2.866   **B.** 2.146   **C.** 3.46   **D.** 2.046   1. _____

2. Find $0.6 - 0.19$.

   A. 0.581   **B.** 0.51   **C.** 0.13   **D.** 0.41   2. _____

3. What is the product of 1.85 and 2.4?

   A. 4.44   **B.** 3.44   **C.** 4.42   **D.** 4.34   3. _____

4. Eight pounds of walnuts costs $43.84. How much does a pound of walnuts cost?

   A. $5.44   **B.** $6.30   **C.** $5.48   **D.** $6.23   4. _____

Skill 2: Factors and Prime Numbers

5. Which number has the prime factorization $2 \times 3 \times 3 \times 5 \times 5$?

   A. 300   **B.** 450   **C.** 900   **D.** 1,125   5. _____

6. Find the prime factorization of 126.

   A. $2 \times 9 \times 7$ **B.** $3 \times 6 \times 7$
   C. $2 \times 3 \times 3 \times 7$ **D.** $2 \times 2 \times 3 \times 7$ 6. _____

7. What is the greatest common factor of 36 and 40?

   A. 8   **B.** 3   **C.** 6   **D.** 4   7. _____

8. A scout troop leader has 18 marshmallows and 24 pieces of chocolate. Both the chocolate and the marshmallows can be divided equally among the troop's members. What is the greatest possible number of members in the troop?

   A. 6   **B.** 8   **C.** 12   **D.** 18   8. _____

GO ON

▬▬ Basic Skills Test, Form B (continued)

Skill 3: Fraction Operations

9. Find $\frac{5}{8} + \frac{1}{6}$.

    A. $1\frac{1}{8}$ **B.** $\frac{3}{7}$ **C.** $\frac{19}{24}$ **D.** $1\frac{7}{24}$ 9. _____

10. Find $6\frac{3}{4} - 3\frac{1}{8}$.

    A. $2\frac{7}{8}$ **B.** $3\frac{7}{8}$ **C.** $3\frac{1}{2}$ **D.** $3\frac{5}{8}$ 10. _____

11. What is the product of $\frac{2}{3}$ and $3\frac{3}{5}$?

    A. $2\frac{2}{5}$ **B.** $2\frac{2}{15}$ **C.** $3\frac{2}{5}$ **D.** $2\frac{3}{5}$ 11. _____

12. Find $\frac{7}{12} \div \frac{3}{4}$.

    A. $\frac{7}{12}$ **B.** $1\frac{5}{16}$ **C.** $\frac{7}{9}$ **D.** $\frac{7}{16}$ 12. _____

Skill 4: Exponent Awareness

13. Simplify the expression $(12 - 6)^2$.

    A. 6   **B.** 36   **C.** 0   **D.** -6 13. _____

14. Write the expression $0.3 \times 0.3 \times 0.3 \times 0.3 \times 0.3$ using exponents.

    A. $4^{0.3}$ **B.** 0.3^5 **C.** 0.3^4 **D.** $10^{0.3}$ 14. _____

15. Simplify the expression $(-5)^4$.

    A. 625   **B.** 20   **C.** -20 **D.** -625 15. _____

16. Which expression represents the volume of a cube whose edge length is 20 units?

    A. 3^{20} **B.** 3^{10} **C.** 20^3 **D.** $3(20)$ 16. _____

GO ON ⇨

Basic Skills Test, Form B (continued)

Skill 5: Proportional Reasoning

17. Which ratio is *not* equivalent to the others?

    A. 3 : 4   **B.** 6 : 8   **C.** 4 : 7   **D.** 9 : 12   17. _____

18. What is the missing term in the proportion $\frac{y}{18} = \frac{16}{24}$?

    A. 6   **B.** 12   **C.** 9   **D.** 42   18. _____

19. Below are two similar figures. Find x.

    A. 100
    B. 80
    C. 60
    D. 50   19. _____

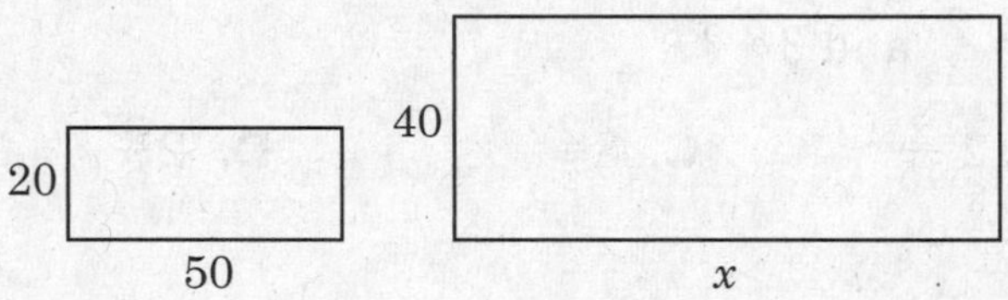

(Figure: small rectangle labeled 20 on the left side and 50 on the bottom; larger rectangle labeled 40 on the left side and x on the bottom.)

20. A map has a scale of 1 cm : 1,000 km. How many centimeters on the map represents 3,500 km?

    A. 35 cm   **B.** 0.3 cm   **C.** 3.5 cm   **D.** 3 cm   20. _____

Skill 6: Percents

21. Convert $\frac{1}{3}$ to percent. Round to the nearest tenth.

    A. 33.3%   **B.** 3%   **C.** 3.3%   **D.** 30%   21. _____

22. Which group does *not* consist of equivalent numbers?

    A. $\frac{5}{20}$, 0.25, 25%   **B.** $\frac{5}{12}$, 0.4, 40%

    C. $\frac{15}{10}$, 1.5, 150%   **D.** $\frac{4}{8}$, 0.5, 50%   22. _____

23. Suppose the sales tax rate is 7%. How much sales tax would be charged for an item priced at $70.00?

    A. $4.90   **B.** $10.00   **C.** $.49   **D.** $1.00   23. _____

24. 60 is 20% of what number?

    A. 12   **B.** 30   **C.** 120   **D.** 300   24. _____

GO ON ▷

Basic Skills Test, Form B (continued)

Skill 7: Finding Perimeter, Area, and Volume

25. Find the perimeter and area of a rectangle 4 in. wide and 5 in. long.
    - **A.** 18 in. and 10 in.²
    - **B.** 9 in. and 10 in.²
    - **C.** 18 in. and 20 in.²
    - **D.** 9 in. and 20 in.²

    25. _____

26. What is the area of the triangle?
    - **A.** 24 m²
    - **B.** 30 m²
    - **C.** 40 m²
    - **D.** 48 m²

    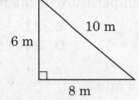

    26. _____

27. The formula for the area of a circle is πr^2. Find the radius of a circle whose area is 12.56 cm².
    - **A.** 40 cm
    - **B.** 2 cm
    - **C.** 20 cm
    - **D.** 4 cm

    27. _____

28. What is the volume of a rectangular prism with length 10 ft, width 6 ft, and height 4 ft?
    - **A.** 20 ft³
    - **B.** 60 ft³
    - **C.** 216 ft³
    - **D.** 240 ft³

    28. _____

Skill 8: Integer Awareness

29. Choose the true statement.
    - **A.** $3 < -5$
    - **B.** $-8 > -6$
    - **C.** $-4 > 0$
    - **D.** $-2 < 2$

    29. _____

30. In January, the temperature in Thule, Greenland ranges from $-50°F$ to $3°F$. Which temperature is *not* likely to be measured in Thule?
    - **A.** $-55°F$
    - **B.** $0°F$
    - **C.** $-45°F$
    - **D.** $-2°F$

    30. _____

31. Order the integers 4, −11, 0, 15, 17, and −2 from least to greatest.
    - **A.** $-11, -2, 0, 4, 15, 17$
    - **B.** $0, -2, 4, -11, 15, 17$
    - **C.** $-2, -11, 0, 4, 15, 17$
    - **D.** $17, 15, -11, 4, -2, 0$

    31. _____

32. Which expression is *not* equivalent to the opposite of $+5$?
    - **A.** $-|-5|$
    - **B.** $|-5|$
    - **C.** -5
    - **D.** $-|5|$

    32. _____

GO ON

▄▄▄▄ Basic Skills Test, Form B (continued)

Skill 9: Integer Operations

33. Find the value of the expression $8 - 16 + (-8)$.

    A. 0   **B.** 16   **C.** −16   **D.** 8   **33.** _____

34. One night the temperature outside was 24°F. The temperature dropped 32°F overnight. Which expression can you use to find the temperature in the morning?

    A. $-32 + (-24)$ **B.** $32 - (-24)$

    C. $24 - (-32)$ **D.** $24 + (-32)$ **34.** _____

35. What is the product of −3 and −70?

    A. 210   **B.** 240   **C.** −240   **D.** −210   **35.** _____

36. Find $200 \div (-25)$.

    A. −4   **B.** −8   **C.** 175   **D.** 8   **36.** _____

Skill 10: Translating Words into Mathematical Expressions

37. Which variable expression corresponds to "6 less than a number"?

    A. $x - 6$ **B.** $x \div 6$ **C.** $6 - x$ **D.** $x + 6$ **37.** _____

38. Which word phrase could correspond to the variable expression $\frac{n}{10}$?

    A. a number decreased by 10   **B.** 10 divided by a number

    C. 10 times a number   **D.** a number divided by 10   **38.** _____

39. Write a variable expression that corresponds to "the product of 8 and m."

    A. $8 + m$ **B.** $8m$ **C.** $8 \div m$ **D.** $8 - m$ **39.** _____

40. A bottling machine can fill b bottles per minute. Which variable expression represents the number of bottles that can be filled in 20 minutes?

    A. $\frac{b}{20}$ **B.** $20 + b$ **C.** $20b$ **D.** $b - 20$ **40.** _____

GO ON ⟹

Basic Skills Test, Form B (continued)

Skill 11: Solving One-Step Equations

41. Solve $m - 5 = -4$.

    A. 9   **B.** -9 **C.** 1   **D.** -1 **41.** _____

42. Solve $p + 2 = -6$.

    A. 8   **B.** 4   **C.** -4 **D.** -8 **42.** _____

43. Solve $72 = -8t$.

    A. 8   **B.** -9 **C.** 9   **D.** -8 **43.** _____

44. Solve $\dfrac{x}{-4} = -20$.

    A. 5   **B.** -80 **C.** 80   **D.** -5 **44.** _____

STOP

Basic Skills Test, Form C

Skill 1: Decimal Operations

1. Find $4.088 + 0.05$.

   A. 4.588   **B.** 4.93   **C.** 4.038   **D.** 4.138   1. _____

2. Find $0.8 - 0.19$.

   A. 0.61   **B.** 0.71   **C.** 0.781   **D.** 0.11   2. _____

3. What is the product of 1.54 and 2.5?

   A. 3.85   **B.** 3.63   **C.** 3.70   **D.** 3.75   3. _____

4. Six pounds of dried figs costs $40.68. How much does one pound of dried figs cost?

   A. $6.93   **B.** $6.78   **C.** $7.12   **D.** $5.82   4. _____

Skill 2: Factors and Prime Numbers

5. Which number has the prime factorization $2 \times 2 \times 3 \times 5 \times 5$?

   A. 140   **B.** 150   **C.** 300   **D.** 120   5. _____

6. Find the prime factorization of 315.

   A. $2 \times 3 \times 3 \times 5$ **B.** $3 \times 3 \times 5 \times 7$

   C. $5 \times 9 \times 7$ **D.** $2 \times 3 \times 5 \times 7$ 6. _____

7. What is the greatest common factor of 36 and 45?

   A. 3   **B.** 6   **C.** 9   **D.** 15   7. _____

8. A group of friends have collected 100 regular baseball cards and 16 special edition cards. Each set of cards can be divided equally among the friends. What is the greatest possible number of friends in the group?

   A. 2   **B.** 4   **C.** 8   **D.** 10   8. _____

GO ON ⟶

Basic Skills Test, Form C (continued)

Skill 3: Fraction Operations

9. Find $\frac{7}{8} + \frac{1}{6}$.

    A. $1\frac{4}{7}$ **B.** $1\frac{1}{14}$ **C.** $\frac{25}{48}$ **D.** $1\frac{1}{24}$ **9.** _____

10. Find $6\frac{4}{5} - 2\frac{3}{10}$.

    A. $4\frac{1}{5}$ **B.** $4\frac{1}{2}$ **C.** $3\frac{9}{10}$ **D.** $4\frac{1}{10}$ **10.** _____

11. What is the product of $\frac{2}{3}$ and $4\frac{1}{5}$?

    A. $2\frac{2}{5}$ **B.** $4\frac{1}{5}$ **C.** $2\frac{4}{5}$ **D.** 2 **11.** _____

12. Find $\frac{5}{12} \div \frac{3}{4}$.

    A. $\frac{5}{9}$ **B.** $\frac{5}{16}$ **C.** $\frac{1}{4}$ **D.** $\frac{1}{3}$ **12.** _____

Skill 4: Exponent Awareness

13. Simplify the expression $(4 - 2)^2$.

    A. 2   **B.** 4   **C.** 0   **D.** -2 **13.** _____

14. Write the expression $0.3 \times 0.3 \times 0.3 \times 0.3 \times 0.3$ using exponents.

    A. 0.3^5 **B.** $5^{0.3}$ **C.** 0.3^4 **D.** $10^{0.3}$ **14.** _____

15. Simplify the expression $(-2)^4$.

    A. -16 **B.** 8   **C.** -8 **D.** 16   **15.** _____

16. Which expression represents the volume of a cube whose edge length is 40 units?

    A. 3^{40} **B.** 40^3 **C.** 3^{40} **D.** $3(40)$ **16.** _____

GO ON

▬▬ Basic Skills Test, Form C (continued)

Skill 5: Proportional Reasoning

17. Which ratio is *not* equivalent to the others?

    A. $2:3$ **B.** $3:4$ **C.** $4:6$ **D.** $10:15$ 17. _____

18. What is the missing term in the proportion $\frac{y}{20} = \frac{18}{24}$?

    A. 12   **B.** 44   **C.** 15   **D.** 16   18. _____

19. Below are two similar figures. Find x.

    A. 15
    B. 30
    C. 40
    D. 60   19. _____

20. A map has a scale of 1 cm : 10 km. How many centimeters on the map represents 50 km?

    A. 50 cm   **B.** 0.5 cm   **C.** 2 cm   **D.** 5 cm   20. _____

Skill 6: Percents

21. Convert $\frac{2}{3}$ to percent. Round to the nearest tenth.

    A. 66.7%   **B.** 3%   **C.** 1.5%   **D.** 6.7%   21. _____

22. Which group does *not* consist of equivalent numbers?

    A. $\frac{2}{20}$, 0.1, 10%   **B.** $\frac{46}{10}$, 4.6, 460%

    C. $\frac{3}{8}$, 0.3, 30%   **D.** $\frac{2}{8}$, 0.25, 25%   22. _____

23. Suppose the sales tax rate is 4%. How much sales tax would be charged for an item priced at $80.00?

    A. $2.00   **B.** $3.20   **C.** $.32   **D.** $20.00   23. _____

24. 70 is 20% of what number?

    A. 35   **B.** 14   **C.** 140   **D.** 350   24. _____

GO ON ⇨

Basic Skills Test, Form C (continued)

Skill 7: Finding Perimeter, Area, and Volume

25. Find the perimeter and area of a rectangle 5 in. wide and 6 in. long.

   A. 11 in. and 15 in.²   **B.** 22 in. and 15 in.²

   C. 11 in. and 30 in.²   **D.** 22 in. and 30 in.²   **25.** _____

26. What is the area of the triangle?

   A. 192 m²

   B. 96 m²

   C. 48 m²

   D. 120 m²   **26.** _____

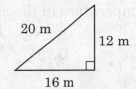

27. The formula for the area of a circle is πr^2. Find the radius of a circle whose area is 78.5 cm².

   A. 5 cm   **B.** 50 cm   **C.** 10 cm   **D.** 25 cm   **27.** _____

28. What is the volume of a rectangular prism with length 10 ft, width 6 ft, and height 3 ft?

   A. 216 ft³   **B.** 180 ft³   **C.** 60 ft³   **D.** 19 ft³   **28.** _____

Skill 8: Integer Awareness

29. Choose the true statement.

   A. $-1 > 1$ **B.** $5 < -6$ **C.** $-5 < -2$ **D.** $0 < -3$ **29.** _____

30. The forecast for North Cape, Norway is for a low of $-28°C$ and a high of $-4°C$. Which temperature is *not* likely to be measured in North Cape?

   A. $0°C$ **B.** $-16°C$ **C.** $-6°C$ **D.** $-27°C$ **30.** _____

31. Order the integers $-3, 16, 0, -6, 20,$ and 8 from least to greatest.

   A. $0, -3, -6, 8, 16, 20$ **B.** $-6, -3, 0, 8, 16, 20$

   C. $-3, -6, 0, 8, 16, 20$ **D.** $20, 16, 8, 0, -3, -6$ **31.** _____

32. Which expression is *not* equivalent to the opposite of $+6$?

   A. $-|-6|$ **B.** $-|6|$ **C.** -6 **D.** $|-6|$ **32.** _____

Basic Skills Test, Form C (continued)

Skill 9: Integer Operations

33. Find the value of the expression $5 - 10 + (-5)$.

    A. -10 **B.** 0 **C.** 10 **D.** 5 33. _____

34. One night the temperature outside was $12°C$. The temperature dropped $18°C$ overnight. Which expression can you use to find the temperature in the morning?

    A. $12 - (-18)$ **B.** $-18 + (-12)$
    C. $12 + (-18)$ **D.** $18 + (-12)$ 34. _____

35. What is the product of -4 and -80?

    A. -320 **B.** 280 **C.** -280 **D.** 320 35. _____

36. Find $250 \div (-25)$.

    A. -5 **B.** -10 **C.** 10 **D.** -25 36. _____

Skill 10: Translating Words into Mathematical Expressions

37. Which variable expression corresponds to "8 less than a number"?

    A. $8 - x$ **B.** $x + 8$ **C.** $x - 8$ **D.** $x \div 8$ 37. _____

38. Which word phrase could correspond to the variable expression $\frac{n}{12}$?

    A. a number divided by 12   **B.** 12 divided by a number
    C. 12 times a number   **D.** a number decreased by 12   38. _____

39. Write a variable expression that corresponds to "the product of 5 and r."

    A. $5 + r$ **B.** $5r$ **C.** $5 \div r$ **D.** $5 - r$ 39. _____

40. Wire costs w dollars per yard. Which variable expression represents the cost of 4 yards of wire?

    A. $\frac{w}{4}$ **B.** $4 + w$ **C.** $4w$ **D.** $w - 4$ 40. _____

GO ON ⇒

Algebra Readiness Tests

Basic Skills Test, Form C (continued)

Skill 11: Solving One-Step Equations

41. Solve $b - 3 = -2$.

    A. -1 **B.** 5   **C.** -5 **D.** 1   **41.** _____

42. Solve $w + 5 = -4$.

    A. -9 **B.** 1   **C.** -1 **D.** 9   **42.** _____

43. Solve $48 = -6z$.

    A. 7   **B.** -7 **C.** -8 **D.** 8   **43.** _____

44. Solve $\dfrac{a}{-3} = -15$.

    A. -5 **B.** 5   **C.** -45 **D.** 45   **44.** _____

STOP

Basic Skills Test, Form D

Skill 1: Decimal Operations

1. Find 3.055 + 0.06.
   A. 3.115   **B.** 4.15   **C.** 3.015   **D.** 3.655   1. _____

2. Find 0.4 − 0.18.
   A. 0.382   **B.** 0.14   **C.** 0.22   **D.** 0.32   2. _____

3. What is the product of 1.94 and 2.5?
   A. 4.83   **B.** 4.65   **C.** 4.75   **D.** 4.85   3. _____

4. Eight gallons of gas costs $9.36. How much does one gallon of gas cost?
   A. $1.17   **B.** $1.07   **C.** $1.22   **D.** $1.02   4. _____

Skill 2: Factors and Prime Numbers

5. Which number has the prime factorization $2 \times 2 \times 3 \times 3 \times 5$?
   A. 60   **B.** 180   **C.** 270   **D.** 90   5. _____

6. Find the prime factorization of 140.
   A. $2 \times 3 \times 5 \times 9$ **B.** $2 \times 5 \times 5 \times 7$
   C. $2 \times 2 \times 5 \times 7$ **D.** $2 \times 2 \times 3 \times 5$ 6. _____

7. What is the greatest common factor of 16 and 100?
   A. 2   **B.** 4   **C.** 8   **D.** 25   7. _____

8. The local model airplane club has a set of 27 biplanes and a set of 36 single-wing airplanes. Each set can be divided equally among the club's members. What is the greatest possible number of members?
   A. 3   **B.** 4   **C.** 6   **D.** 9   8. _____

GO ON ⟹

Basic Skills Test, Form D (continued)

Skill 3: Fraction Operations

9. Find $\frac{7}{8} + \frac{5}{6}$.

   A. $1\frac{17}{24}$ **B.** $\frac{6}{7}$ **C.** $1\frac{3}{4}$ **D.** $1\frac{2}{3}$ 9. _____

10. Find $5\frac{3}{5} - 3\frac{3}{10}$.

   A. $2\frac{3}{5}$ **B.** $1\frac{3}{10}$ **C.** $2\frac{3}{10}$ **D.** $2\frac{7}{10}$ 10. _____

11. What is the product of $\frac{3}{4}$ and $2\frac{2}{5}$?

   A. $2\frac{3}{10}$ **B.** $1\frac{3}{10}$ **C.** $1\frac{3}{5}$ **D.** $1\frac{4}{5}$ 11. _____

12. Find $\frac{3}{10} \div \frac{2}{5}$.

   A. $\frac{3}{25}$ **B.** $\frac{3}{10}$ **C.** $\frac{3}{4}$ **D.** $\frac{6}{25}$ 12. _____

Skill 4: Exponent Awareness

13. Simplify the expression $(10 - 5)^2$.

   A. 25   **B.** -5 **C.** 5   **D.** 0   13. _____

14. Write the expression $0.4 \times 0.4 \times 0.4 \times 0.4 \times 0.4$ using exponents.

   A. $10^{0.4}$ **B.** 0.4^4 **C.** 0.4^5 **D.** $5^{0.4}$ 14. _____

15. Simplify the expression $(-3)^4$.

   A. -12 **B.** 81   **C.** -81 **D.** 12   15. _____

16. Which expression represents the volume of a cube whose edge length is 30 units?

   A. 3^{30} **B.** 3^{10} **C.** $3(30)$ **D.** 30^3 16. _____

GO ON ⇒

Basic Skills Test, Form D (continued)

Skill 5: Proportional Reasoning

17. Which ratio is *not* equivalent to the others?

   A. $4:5$ **B.** $5:7$ **C.** $12:15$ **D.** $8:10$ **17.**_____

18. What is the missing term in the proportion $\frac{y}{12} = \frac{15}{20}$?

   A. 10   **B.** 6   **C.** 32   **D.** 9   **18.**_____

19. Below are two similar figures. Find x.

   A. 10
   B. 15
   C. 20
   D. 30

   10 ▭ x ▭
       30   60   **19.**_____

20. A map has a scale of 1 cm : 1,000 m. How many centimeters on the map represents 1,500 m?

   A. 1.5 cm   **B.** 0.67 cm   **C.** 6.7 cm   **D.** 15 cm   **20.**_____

Skill 6: Percents

21. Convert $\frac{5}{6}$ to percent. Round to the nearest tenth.

   A. 8.3%   **B.** 12%   **C.** 83.3%   **D.** 1.2%   **21.**_____

22. Which group does *not* consist of equivalent numbers?

   A. $\frac{7}{8}$, 0.8, 80%   **B.** $\frac{6}{20}$, 0.3, 30%

   C. $\frac{45}{10}$, 4.5, 450%   **D.** $\frac{3}{12}$, 0.25, 25%   **22.**_____

23. Suppose the sales tax rate is 5%. How much sales tax would be charged for an item priced at $50.00?

   A. $1.00   **B.** $.25   **C.** $10.00   **D.** $2.50   **23.**_____

24. 80 is 40% of what number?

   A. 320   **B.** 200   **C.** 32   **D.** 20   **24.**_____

Basic Skills Test, Form D (continued)

Skill 7: Finding Perimeter, Area, and Volume

25. Find the perimeter and area of a rectangle 5 in. wide and 8 in. long.

    A. 13 in. and 40 in.^{2} **B.** 13 in. and 20 in.^{2}

    C. 26 in. and 40 in.^{2} **D.** 26 in. and 20 in.^{2} 25. _____

26. What is the area of the triangle?

    A. 60 m^2

    B. 300 m^2

    C. 250 m^2

    D. 150 m^2 26. _____

15 m   25 m   20 m

27. The formula for the area of a circle is πr^2. Find the radius of a circle whose area is 50.24 cm^2.

    A. 16 cm   **B.** 4 cm   **C.** 8 cm   **D.** 40 cm   27. _____

28. What is the volume of a rectangular prism with length 8 ft, width 5 ft, and height 4 ft?

    A. 160 ft^3 **B.** 125 ft^3 **C.** 40 ft^3 **D.** 17 ft^3 28. _____

Skill 8: Integer Awareness

29. Choose the true statement.

    A. $-3 > 2$ **B.** $-2 < 3$ **C.** $0 < -2$ **D.** $-4 > 4$ 29. _____

30. The temperature in the Yukon Territory usually ranges from $-42°C$ to $-2°C$ in December. Which temperature is *not* likely to be measured in the Yukon Territory in December?

    A. $-41°F$ **B.** $-10°C$ **C.** $-6°C$ **D.** $0°C$ 30. _____

31. Order the integers 0, 10, 25, –5, 15, and –1 from least to greatest.

    A. 25, 15, 10, -5, -1, 0   **B.** -1, -5, 0, 10, 15, 25

    C. -5, -1, 0, 10, 15, 25   **D.** 0, -1, -5, 10, 15, 25   31. _____

32. Which expression is *not* equivalent to the opposite of $+2$?

    A. $|-2|$ **B.** -2 **C.** $-|-2|$ **D.** $-|2|$ 32. _____

GO ON ➡

Basic Skills Test, Form D (continued)

Skill 9: Integer Operations

33. Find the value of the expression $4 - 8 + (-4)$.

    A. 4   **B.** -8 **C.** 8   **D.** 0   33. _____

34. One night the temperature outside was 17°F. The temperature dropped 26°F overnight. Which expression can you use to find the temperature in the morning?

    A. $17 - (-26)$ **B.** $26 + (-17)$

    C. $-26 + (-17)$ **D.** $17 + (-26)$ 34. _____

35. What is the product of -4 and -60?

    A. -240 **B.** 240   **C.** 260   **D.** -260 35. _____

36. Find $100 \div (-20)$.

    A. -5 **B.** -20 **C.** 80   **D.** 5   36. _____

Skill 10: Translating Words into Mathematical Expressions

37. Which variable expression corresponds to "2 less than a number"?

    A. $2 - x$ **B.** $x - 2$ **C.** $x \div 2$ **D.** $x + 2$ 37. _____

38. Which word phrase could correspond to the variable expression $\frac{n}{8}$?

    A. 8 times a number   **B.** a number decreased by 8

    C. a number divided by 8   **D.** 8 divided by a number   38. _____

39. Write a variable expression that corresponds to "the product of 10 and r."

    A. $10r$ **B.** $10 \div r$ **C.** $10 - r$ **D.** $10 + r$ 39. _____

40. A bakery bakes b bagels per day. Which variable expression represents the number of bagels baked in 6 days?

    A. $6 + b$ **B.** $6b$ **C.** $b - 6$ **D.** $\frac{b}{6}$ 40. _____

GO ON →

Basic Skills Test, Form D (continued)

Skill 11: Solving One-Step Equations

41. Solve $w - 6 = -2$.

   A. -4 **B.** 4   **C.** 8   **D.** -8 **41.** _____

42. Solve $x + 3 = -6$.

   A. -6 **B.** 9   **C.** -9 **D.** -6 **42.** _____

43. Solve $42 = -6t$.

   A. -7 **B.** 8   **C.** -8 **D.** 7   **43.** _____

44. Solve $\dfrac{n}{-3} = -18$.

   A. 6   **B.** 54   **C.** -54 **D.** -6 **44.** _____

STOP

Algebra Concept-Readiness Test, Form A

Concept 1: The Distributive Property

Study the concept, and then answer the test questions on the next page.

You can use the distributive property to simplify an expression in which a sum or a difference inside parentheses is multiplied by a term outside the parentheses.

Distributive Property	
Arithmetic:	Algebra:
$8(5 + 3) = 8(5) + 8(3)$	$a(b + c) = a(b) + a(c)$
$8(5 - 3) = 8(5) - 8(3)$	$a(b - c) = a(b) - a(c)$

Example 1
Use the distributive property to simplify $3(x - 6)$.

$$
\begin{aligned}
3(x - 6) &= 3(x) - 3(6) \\
&= 3x - 18
\end{aligned}
$$

Example 2
Use the distributive property to simplify $7m + 9m$.

$$
\begin{aligned}
7m + 9m &= (7 + 9)m \\
&= (16)m \\
&= 16m
\end{aligned}
$$

Go on to the test questions on the next page.

GO ON ⇒

Algebra Readiness Tests

Algebra Concept-Readiness Test, Form A (continued)

Concept 1: The Distributive Property

Choose the best answer.

1. Find the missing term represented by □:
   $2(7 + 9) = 2(7) + 2(□)$.

   A. 2   **B.** 7   **C.** 9   **D.** 18   1. _____

2. Find the missing term represented by □:
   $10(n + 1) = 10(□) + 10(1)$.

   A. 1   **B.** 10   **C.** n **D.** $n + 1$ 2. _____

3. Simplify $5(5 - y)$.

   A. $25 - y$ **B.** $55 - 5y$ **C.** $25 - 5y$ **D.** $24y$ 3. _____

4. Find the missing term represented by □:
   $□(p + 9) = 11p + 99$.

   A. p **B.** $11p$ **C.** 9   **D.** 11   4. _____

5. Find the missing term represented by □:
   $8x - 3x = (8 - □)x$.

   A. 3   **B.** $3x$ **C.** x **D.** 5   5. _____

6. Simplify $4t + 6t$.

   A. $10 + t$ **B.** $24t$ **C.** $4(t + 6)$ **D.** $10t$ 6. _____

Go on to Concept 2.

GO ON ➡

Algebra Concept-Readiness Test, Form A (continued)

Concept 2: Square Roots

Study the concept, and then answer the test questions on the next page.

To find the square of a number, you multiply the number by itself. The inverse of squaring a number is finding its square roots. The symbol $\sqrt{}$ is used to indicate the positive square root.

Example 1
Find $\sqrt{9}$.

Since $3^2 = 9$, the positive square root of 9 is 3, and $\sqrt{9} = 3$.

A number like 9 that is the square of an integer is called a *perfect square.* If a number is not a perfect square, you can estimate its square root by comparing the square root to consecutive whole numbers.

Example 2
Find two consecutive whole numbers that $\sqrt{55}$ is between.

The consecutive perfect squares that 55 is between are 49 and 64.

$$49 \le 55 \le 64$$
$$\sqrt{49} \le \sqrt{55} \le \sqrt{64}$$
$$7 \le \sqrt{55} \le 8$$

So, $\sqrt{55}$ is between 7 and 8.

Go on to the test questions on the next page.

GO ON

Algebra Concept-Readiness Test, Form A (continued)

Concept 2: Square Roots

Choose the best answer.

7. Find $\sqrt{16}$.
   A. 4 **B.** 2 **C.** 16 **D.** 8   7. _____

8. Find $\sqrt{144}$.
   A. 14 **B.** 12 **C.** 72 **D.** 13   8. _____

9. Which number's square is equal to its positive square root?
   A. 25 **B.** 4 **C.** 1 **D.** 10   9. _____

10. If $\sqrt{c} = 9$, what is the value of c?
    A. 81 **B.** 3 **C.** 9 **D.** 18   10. _____

11. Find two consecutive whole numbers that $\sqrt{40}$ is between.
    A. 2 and 3 **B.** 9 and 10 **C.** 4 and 5 **D.** 6 and 7   11. _____

12. Which statement is *not* true?
    A. $1 < \sqrt{3} < 2$ **B.** $2 < \sqrt{10} < 3$
    C. $3 < \sqrt{12} < 4$ **D.** $4 < \sqrt{20} < 5$ 12. _____

Go on to Concept 3.

GO ON ⇒

Algebra Concept-Readiness Test, Form A (continued)

Concept 3: Writing Equations

Study the concept, and then answer the test questions on the next page.

You can translate a word phrase into a *variable expression*. A variable expression is a group of numbers, variables, and operations. Here are some examples.

Word Phrase	Variable Expression
the sum of m and 45	$m + 45$
22 more than a number	$n + 22$
w less than 55	$55 - w$
the product of w and 10	$10w$
the quotient of r and s	$r \div s$

You can translate the words of a problem into the symbols of an equation.

Example
The diameter of Saturn is about 17 times the diameter of Mars. The diameter of Saturn is about 71,000 mi. Write an equation you can use to find the approximate diameter of Mars.

Let m = diameter of Mars.

Words	diameter of Saturn	is	17	times	diameter of Mars
	↓	↓	↓	↓	↓
Equation	71,000	=	17	×	m

So, you can use the equation $71,000 = 17m$ to find the approximate diameter of Mars.

Go on to the test questions on the next page.

GO ON ⟩

Algebra Concept-Readiness Test, Form A (continued)

Concept 3: Writing Equations

Choose the best answer.

13. Choose the variable expression that represents the quantity ten less than x.

    A. $10 - x$ **B.** $10x$ **C.** $x - 10$ **D.** $10 + x$ 13._____

14. Which variable expression represents the quotient of g and 3?

    A. $\frac{g}{3}$ **B.** $g \times 3$ **C.** $3 \div g$ **D.** $3 \times g$ 14._____

15. There are c compact discs on each shelf. Write a variable expression that represents the number of compact discs on 25 shelves.

    A. $25 + c$ **B.** $25 \div c$ **C.** $25c$ **D.** $25 - c$ 15._____

16. The product of -6 and an unknown number is -60. Which equation describes this relationship?

    A. $\frac{x}{-60} = -6$ **B.** $-60x = -6$

    C $\frac{-6}{x} = -60$ **D.** $-6x = -60$ 16._____

17. This season, the Jays won eight fewer games than the Hawks. The Jays won 33 games. Choose the equation you could use to find the number of games the Hawks won.

    A. $33 - h = 8$ **B.** $33 = h - 8$

    C. $h + j = 33$ **D.** $h + 33 = 8$ 17._____

18. Suppose you travel at an average rate of 30 miles per hour. Which equation would you use to find the time it takes to travel 575 miles?

    A. $575t = 30$ **B.** $t = \frac{30}{575}$

    C. $\frac{t}{575} = 30$ **D.** $30t = 575$ 18._____

GO ON

Go on to Concept 4.

Algebra Concept-Readiness Test, Form A (continued)

Concept 4: Solving Equations Using the Properties of Equality

Study the concept, and then answer the test questions on the next page.

You can use the Properties of Equality to solve equations.

Properties of Equality	
Addition	You can add the same value to each side of an equation.
Subtraction	You can subtract the same value from each side of an equation.
Multiplication	You can multiply each side of an equation by the same value.
Division	You can divide each side of an equation by the same nonzero value.

Example 1

Solve $x - 5 = -11$.

$$x - 5 = -11$$
$$x - 5 + 5 = -11 + 5 \qquad \leftarrow \textbf{Add 5 to each side of the equation.}$$
$$x + 0 = -6 \qquad \leftarrow \textbf{Simplify.}$$
$$x = -6 \qquad \leftarrow \textbf{Simplify.}$$

Example 2

Solve $4x + 3 = 39$.

$$4x + 3 = 39$$
$$4x + 3 - 3 = 39 - 3 \qquad \leftarrow \textbf{Subtract 3 from each side of the equation.}$$
$$4x = 36$$
$$\frac{4x}{4} = \frac{36}{4} \qquad \leftarrow \textbf{Divide each side of the equation by 4.}$$
$$x = 9 \qquad \leftarrow \textbf{Simplify.}$$

Go on to the test questions on the next page.

GO ON ⇨

Algebra Readiness Tests

Algebra Concept-Readiness Test, Form A (continued)

Concept 4: Solving Equations Using the Properties of Equality

Choose the best answer.

19. Solve $m - 5 = 12$.
   A. 7   **B.** 15   **C.** −7   **D.** 17   19._____

20. Solve $20 = d + (-5)$.
   A. 25   **B.** 15   **C.** −25   **D.** −15   20._____

21. Solve $-4t = 28$.
   A. 14   **B.** –7   **C.** 7   **D.** $-\frac{1}{7}$ 21._____

22. Solve $\frac{r}{3} = 27$.
   A. 9   **B.** $\frac{1}{9}$ **C.** 81   **D.** 61   22._____

23. Solve $5y - 10 = -20$.
   A. 6   **B.** −2   **C.** 2   **D.** −6   23._____

24. Solve $\frac{d}{4} + 3 = 5$.
   A. 8   **B.** 32   **C.** 2   **D.** –8   24._____

Go on to Concept 5.

GO ON

Algebra Concept-Readiness Test, Form A (continued)

Concept 5: Graphing Solutions of Equations

Study the concept, and then answer the test questions on the next page.

An ordered pair whose values make an equation true is a *solution* of the equation.

Example 1
Determine whether the ordered pair $(-2, 0)$ is a solution of the equation $y = x + 2$.

$$y = x + 2$$
Substitute 0 for y. → $0 \overset{?}{=} -2 + 2$ ← **Substitute −2 for x.**
$$0 = 0 \checkmark$$

$0 = 0$, so $(-2, 0)$ is a solution of $y = x + 2$.

You can graph the solutions of an equation on the coordinate plane.

Example 2
Graph four solutions of the equation $y = 3x - 4$.

Step 1: Make a table to find solutions.

Step 2: Graph the solutions.

Choose four values for x.
↓   **Substitute and simplify.**

x	$3x - 4 = y$	(x, y)
0	$3(0) - 4 = -4$	$(0, -4)$
1	$3(1) - 4 = -1$	$(1, -1)$
2	$3(2) - 4 = 2$	$(2, 2)$
3	$3(3) - 4 = 5$	$(3, 5)$

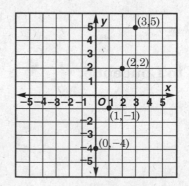

Go on to the test questions on the next page.

GO ON

Algebra Concept-Readiness Test, Form A (continued)

Concept 5: Graphing Solutions of Equations

Choose the best answer.

25. Which is a solution of the equation $y = x - 3$?

    A. $(2, 1)$ **B.** $(-1, -4)$ **C.** $(0, 3)$ **D.** $(3, 6)$ **25.** _____

26. Which is a solution of the equation $y = 12x$?

    A. $(0, 0)$ **B.** $(12, 1)$ **C.** $(1, 1)$ **D.** $(3, 4)$ **26.** _____

27. Find the missing term represented by □:

x	$x - 3$	y	(x, y)
-1	$-1 - 3$	-4	$(-1, -4)$
0	$0 - 3$	-3	$(0, -3)$
□	□ $- 3$	-2	$(□, -2)$

    A. 2   **B.** 0   **C.** 3   **D.** 1   **27.** _____

28. Which is a solution of the equation $y = 2x + 8$?

    A. $(0, 0)$ **B.** $(1, 11)$ **C.** $(2, 10)$ **D.** $(3, 14)$ **28.** _____

29. Which is NOT a solution of the equation $y = 4x - 1$?

    A. $(0, 1)$ **B.** $(2, 7)$ **C.** $(1, 3)$ **D.** $(-1, -5)$ **29.** _____

30. Which graph shows solutions of the equation $y = 3x - 1$?

A.
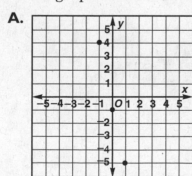

B.
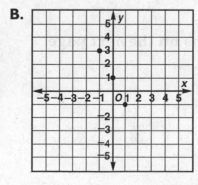

C.
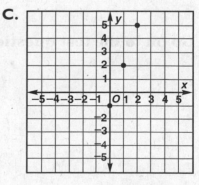

    30. _____

▀▀▀▀Algebra Concept-Readiness Test, Form B

Concept 1: The Distributive Property

Study the concept, and then answer the test questions on the next page.

You can use the distributive property to simplify an expression in which a sum or a difference inside parentheses is multiplied by a term outside the parentheses.

Distributive Property	
Arithmetic:	Algebra:
$8(5 + 3) = 8(5) + 8(3)$	$a(b + c) = a(b) + a(c)$
$8(5 - 3) = 8(5) - 8(3)$	$a(b - c) = a(b) - a(c)$

Example 1
Use the distributive property to simplify $3(x - 6)$.

$$3(x - 6) = 3(x) - 3(6)$$
$$= 3x - 18$$

Example 2
Use the distributive property to simplify $7m + 9m$.

$$7m + 9m = (7 + 9)m$$
$$= (16)m$$
$$= 16m$$

Go on to the test questions on the next page.

GO ON ▷

▬▬Algebra Concept-Readiness Test, Form B (continued)

Concept 1: The Distributive Property

Choose the best answer.

1. Find the missing term represented by □:
   3(5 + 8) = 3(5) + 3 (□).
   A. 3   **B.** 5   **C.** 8   **D.** 24   1. _____

2. Find the missing term represented by □:
   5(x + 2) = 5(□) + 5 (2).
   A. x **B.** $x + 2$ **C.** 5   **D.** 2   2. _____

3. Simplify 4(4 − n).
   A. $15n$ **B.** $44 − 4n$ **C.** $16 − 4n$ **D.** $16 − n$ 3. _____

4. Find the missing term represented by □:
   □(t + 7) = 10t + 70.
   A. 7   **B.** 10   **C.** t **D.** $10t$ 4. _____

5. Find the missing term represented by □:
   7y − 5y = (7 − □)y.
   A. $2y$ **B.** y **C.** 2   **D.** 5   5. _____

6. Simplify 5p + 8p.
   A. $13p$ **B.** $40p$ **C.** $13 + p$ **D.** $5(p + 8)$ 6. _____

Go on to Concept 2.

GO ON ⟩

Algebra Concept-Readiness Test, Form B (continued)

Concept 2: Square Roots

Study the concept, and then answer the test questions on the next page.

To find the square of a number, you multiply the number by itself. The inverse of squaring a number is finding its square roots. The symbol $\sqrt{}$ is used to indicate the positive square root.

Example 1
Find $\sqrt{9}$.

Since $3^2 = 9$, the positive square root of 9 is 3, and $\sqrt{9} = 3$.

A number like 9 that is the square of an integer is called a *perfect square*. If a number is not a perfect square, you can estimate its square root by comparing the square root to consecutive whole numbers.

Example 2
Find two consecutive whole numbers that $\sqrt{55}$ is between.

The consecutive perfect squares that 55 is between are 49 and 64.

$$49 \ < \ 55 \ < \ 64$$
$$\sqrt{49} < \sqrt{55} < \sqrt{64}$$
$$7 \ \ < \sqrt{55} \ < \ \ 8$$

So, $\sqrt{55}$ is between 7 and 8.

Go on to the test questions on the next page.

GO ON

Algebra Concept-Readiness Test, Form B *(continued)*

Concept 2: Square Roots

Choose the best answer.

7. Find $\sqrt{36}$.
   A. 36   **B.** 18   **C.** 6   **D.** 3   7. _____

8. Find $\sqrt{121}$.
   A. 12   **B.** 11   **C.** 121   **D.** 60.5   8. _____

9. Which number's positive square root is equal to its square?
   A. 1   **B.** 9   **C.** 6   **D.** 2   9. _____

10. If $\sqrt{b} = 4$, what is the value of b?
    A. 2   **B.** 4   **C.** 8   **D.** 16   10. _____

11. Find two consecutive whole numbers that $\sqrt{50}$ is between.
    A. 5 and 6   **B.** 6 and 7   **C.** 7 and 8   **D.** 8 and 9   11. _____

12. Which statement is *not* true?
    A. $2 < \sqrt{5} < 3$ **B.** $4 < \sqrt{17} < 5$
    C. $3 < \sqrt{7} < 4$ **D.** $5 < \sqrt{30} < 6$ 12. _____

Go on to Concept 3.

GO ON

■■■■Algebra Concept-Readiness Test, Form B (continued)

Concept 3: Writing Equations

Study the concept, and then answer the test questions on the next page.

You can translate a word phrase into a *variable expression*. A variable expression is a group of numbers, variables, and operations. Here are some examples.

Word Phrase	Variable Expression
the sum of m and 45	$m + 45$
22 more than a number	$n + 22$
w less than 55	$55 - w$
the product of w and 10	$10w$
the quotient of r and s	$r \div s$

You can translate the words of a problem into the symbols of an equation.

Example
The diameter of Saturn is about 17 times the diameter of Mars. The diameter of Saturn is about 71,000 mi. Write an equation you can use to find the approximate diameter of Mars.

Let m = diameter of Mars.

Words	diameter of Saturn	is	17	times	diameter of Mars
	↓	↓	↓	↓	↓
Equation	71,000	=	17	×	m

So, you can use the equation $71,000 = 17m$ to find the approximate diameter of Mars.

Go on to the test questions on the next page.

GO ON ⟹

Algebra Concept-Readiness Test, Form B (continued)

Concept 3: Writing Equations

Choose the best answer.

13. Choose the variable expression that represents the quantity eight less than y.

    A. 8   **B.** $y - 8$ **C.** $8 - y$ **D.** $8y$ 13. _____

14. Which variable expression represents the quotient of m and 2?

    A. $2 \times m$ **B.** $2 \div m$ **C.** $m \times 2$ **D.** $\frac{m}{2}$ 14. _____

15. There are p passengers in each van. Write a variable expression that represents the number of passengers in 18 vans.

    A. $18p$ **B.** $18 - p$ **C.** $18 + p$ **D.** $18 \div p$ 15. _____

16. The product of -2 and an unknown number is 40. Which equation describes this relationship?

    A. $\frac{-2}{x} = 40$ **B.** $40x = -2$

    C. $-2x = 40$ **D.** $\frac{x}{-2} = 40$ 16. _____

17. This season, the Patriots won six fewer games than the Rebels. The Patriots won 24 games. Choose the equation you could use to find the number of games the Rebels won.

    A. $r + p = 24$ **B.** $r + 24 = 6$

    C. $24 - r = 6$ **D.** $24 = r - 6$ 17. _____

18. Suppose you travel at an average rate of 50 miles per hour. Which equation would you use to find the time it takes to travel 630 miles?

    A. $50t = 630$ **B.** $\frac{t}{630} = 50$

    C. $t = \frac{50}{630}$ **D.** $630t = 50$ 18. _____

Go on to Concept 4.

GO ON →

Algebra Concept-Readiness Test, Form B (continued)

Concept 4: Solving Equations Using the Properties of Equality

Study the concept, and then answer the test questions on the next page.

You can use the Properties of Equality to solve equations.

Properties of Equality	
Addition	You can add the same value to each side of an equation.
Subtraction	You can subtract the same value from each side of an equation.
Multiplication	You can multiply each side of an equation by the same value.
Division	You can divide each side of an equation by the same nonzero value.

Example 1

Solve $x - 5 = -11$.

$$x - 5 = -11$$
$$x - 5 + 5 = -11 + 5 \qquad \leftarrow \textbf{Add 5 to each side of the equation.}$$
$$x + 0 = -6 \qquad \leftarrow \textbf{Simplify.}$$
$$x = -6 \qquad \leftarrow \textbf{Simplify.}$$

Example 2

Solve $4x + 3 = 39$.

$$4x + 3 = 39$$
$$4x + 3 - 3 = 39 - 3 \qquad \leftarrow \textbf{Subtract 3 from each side of the equation.}$$
$$4x = 36$$
$$\frac{4x}{4} = \frac{36}{4} \qquad \leftarrow \textbf{Divide each side of the equation by 4.}$$
$$x = 9 \qquad \leftarrow \textbf{Simplify.}$$

Go on to the test questions on the next page.

GO ON

Algebra Concept-Readiness Test, Form B (continued)

Concept 4: Solving Equations Using the Properties of Equality

Choose the best answer.

19. Solve $p - 7 = 15$.
   A. 22   **B.** 23   **C.** 8   **D.** -8 **19.** _____

20. Solve $14 = m + (-6)$.
   A. 8   **B.** 20   **C.** -20 **D.** -8 **20.** _____

21. Solve $-5x = 30$.
   A. 12   **B.** 6   **C.** -6 **D.** $-\frac{1}{6}$ **21.** _____

22. Solve $\frac{d}{5} = 15$.
   A. 3   **B.** $\frac{1}{3}$ **C.** 55   **D.** 75   **22.** _____

23. Solve $4x - 8 = -20$.
   A. 7   **B.** 3   **C.** -3 **D.** -7 **23.** _____

24. Solve $\frac{m}{3} + 4 = 10$.
   A. 2   **B.** 18   **C.** 42   **D.** -18 **24.** _____

Go on to Concept 5.

GO ON

Algebra Concept-Readiness Test, Form B (continued)

Concept 5: Graphing Solutions of Equations

Study the concept, and then answer the test questions on the next page.

An ordered pair whose values make an equation true is a *solution* of the equation.

Example 1
Determine whether the ordered pair $(-2, 0)$ is a solution of the equation $y = x + 2$.

$$y = x + 2$$
Substitute 0 for y. → $0 \overset{?}{=} -2 + 2$ ← **Substitute -2 for x.**
$$0 = 0 \checkmark$$

$0 = 0$, so $(-2, 0)$ is a solution of $y = x + 2$.

You can graph the solutions of an equation on the coordinate plane.

Example 2
Graph four solutions of the equation $y = 3x - 4$.

Step 1: Make a table to find solutions.   Step 2: Graph the solutions.

Choose four values for x.
↓   **Substitute and simplify.**

x	$3x - 4 = y$	(x, y)
0	$3(0) - 4 = -4$	$(0, -4)$
1	$3(1) - 4 = -1$	$(1, -1)$
2	$3(2) - 4 = 2$	$(2, 2)$
3	$3(3) - 4 = 5$	$(3, 5)$

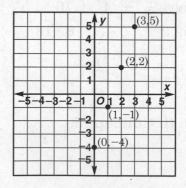

Go on to the test questions on the next page.

GO ON ⇨

Factors and Prime Numbers	5–8			Practice 4-3, 4-4 Reteaching 4-3, 4-4 Enrichment 4-3, 4-4 Computer Test Generator 4-3, 4-4	Practice 2-2 Reteaching 2-2 Enrichment 2-2 Computer Test Generator 2-2	Practice 2-1 Reteaching 2-1 Enrichment 2-1 Computer Test Generator 2-1	Practice 4-3 Reteaching 4-3 Enrichment 4-3 Computer Test Generator 4-3

Parent's or Guardian's signature ______________________

*For Practice Masters, use regular practice (Version A) or adapted practice (Version B).
†For the computer test generator, use the Prentice Hall ExamView Assessment Suite.

Date ______________________

t, Form B (continued)

25. ________

26. ________

D. 9

27. ________

2)

28. ________

−4)

29. ________

30. ________

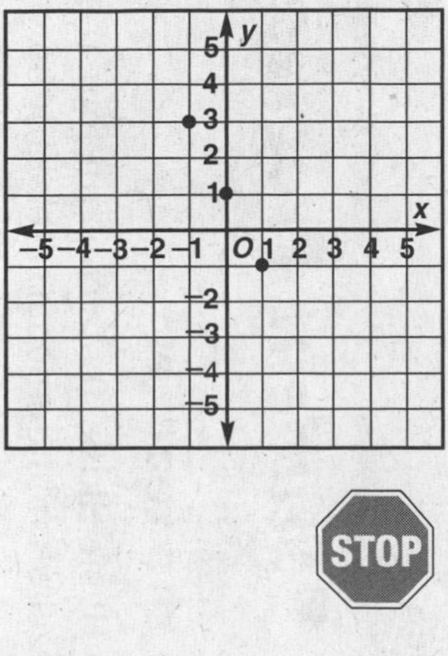

STOP

Student Progress Chart—Basic Skills Test

To the teacher:

The Basic Skills Tests contain four test items for each of the skills listed below. Usually, getting 3 out of 4 correct should demonstrate skill; however, you may wish to set your own criteria.

	Test Items	Number of Items Correct	Demonstrates Skill? (yes or no)	Suggested Remediation *†			
Skill				Prentice Hall Mathematics Course 1	Prentice Hall Mathematics Course 2	Prentice Hall Mathematics Course 3	Prentice Hall Mathematics Pre-Algebra
Decimal Operations	1–4			Practice 1-7, 1-8, 1-9 Reteaching 1-7, 1-8, 1-9 Enrichment 1-7, 1-8, 1-9 Computer Test Generator 1-7, 1-8, 1-9	Practice 1-2, 1-3, 1-4 Reteaching 1-2, 1-3, 1-4 Enrichment 1-2, 1-3, 1-4 Computer Test Generator 1-2, 1-3, 1-4	Student Edition Skills Handbook pp. 631–637	Practice 3-2 Reteaching 3-2 Enrichment 3-2 Computer Test Generator 3-2 Student Edition Skills Handbook pp. 786–792

Student Progress Chart—Basic Skills Test (continued)

Skill	Test Items	Number of Items Correct	Demonstrates Skill? (yes or no)	Suggested Remediation*†			
				Prentice Hall Mathematics Course 1	Prentice Hall Mathematics Course 2	Prentice Hall Mathematics Course 3	Prentice Hall Mathematics Pre-Algebra
Fraction Operations	9–12			Practice 5-1, 5-2, 5-3, 5-4, 5-5, 6-1, 6-2, 6-3, 6-4 Reteaching 5-1, 5-2, 5-3, 5-4, 5-5, 6-1, 6-2, 6-3, 6-4 Enrichment 5-1, 5-2, 5-3, 5-4, 5-5, 6-1, 6-2, 6-3, 6-4 Computer Test Generator 5-1, 5-2, 5-3, 5-4, 5-5, 6-1, 6-2, 6-3, 6-4	Practice 3-2, 3-3, 3-4, 3-5 Reteaching 3-2, 3-3, 3-4, 3-5 Enrichment 3-2, 3-3, 3-4, 3-5 Computer Test Generator 3-2, 3-3, 3-4, 3-5	Practice 2-4, 2-5 Reteaching 2-4, 2-5 Enrichment 2-4, 2-5 Computer Test Generator 2-4, 2-5 Student Edition Skills Handbook p. 639	Practice 5-3, 5-4 Reteaching 5-3, 5-4 Enrichment 5-3, 5-4 Computer Test Generator 5-3, 5-4 Student Edition Skills Handbook p. 795–796
Exponent Awareness	13–16			Practice 4-2 Reteaching 4-2 Enrichment 4-2 Computer Test Generator 4-2	Practice 2-1 Reteaching 2-1 Enrichment 2-1 Computer Test Generator 2-1	Practice 2-7 Reteaching 2-7 Enrichment 2-7 Computer Test Generator 2-7	Practice 4-2 Reteaching 4-2 Enrichment 4-2 Computer Test Generator 4-2
Proportional Reasoning	17–20			Practice 7-1, 7-2, 7-3 Reteaching 7-1, 7-2, 7-3 Enrichment 7-1, 7-2, 7-3 Computer Test Generator 7-1, 7-2, 7-3	Practice 5-1, 5-3, 5-5, 5-6 Reteaching 5-1, 5-3, 5-5, 5-6 Enrichment 5-1, 5-3, 5-5, 5-6 Computer Test Generator 5-1, 5-3, 5-5, 5-6	Practice 4-1, 4-3, 4-4 Reteaching 4-1, 4-3, 4-4 Enrichment 4-1, 4-3, 4-4 Computer Test Generator 4-1, 4-3, 4-4	Practice 6-1, 6-2, 6-3 Reteaching 6-1, 6-2, 6-3 Enrichment 6-1, 6-2, 6-3 Computer Test Generator 6-1, 6-2, 6-3

Student Progress Chart—Basic Skills Test (continued)

Skill	Test Items	Number of Items Correct	Demonstrates Skill? (yes or no)	Suggested Remediation*†			
				Prentice Hall Mathematics Course 1	Prentice Hall Mathematics Course 2	Prentice Hall Mathematics Course 3	Prentice Hall Mathematics Pre-Algebra
Percents	21–24			Practice 7-6, 7-7, 7-8, 7-9 Reteaching 7-6, 7-7, 7-8, 7-9 Enrichment 7-6, 7-7, 7-8, 7-9 Computer Test Generator 7-6, 7-7, 7-8, 7-9	Practice 6-2, 6-3, 6-4, 6-6, 6-7 Reteaching 6-2, 6-3, 6-4, 6-6, 6-7 Enrichment 6-2, 6-3, 6-4, 6-6, 6-7 Computer Test Generator 6-2, 6-3, 6-4, 6-6, 6-7	Practice 5-1, 5-3, 5-4 Reteaching 5-1, 5-3, 5-4 Enrichment 5-1, 5-3, 5-4 Computer Test Generator 5-1, 5-3, 5-4	Practice 6-5, 6-6, 6-7 Reteaching 6-5, 6-6, 6-7 Enrichment 6-5, 6-6, 6-7 Computer Test Generator 6-5, 6-6, 6-7
Finding Perimeter, Area, and Volume	25–28			Practice 9-3, 9-4, 9-6 Reteaching 9-3, 9-4, 9-6 Enrichment 9-3, 9-4, 9-6 Computer Test Generator 9-3, 9-4, 9-6	Practice 8-2, 8-5, 8-10 Reteaching 8-2, 8-5, 8-10 Enrichment 8-2, 8-5, 8-10 Computer Test Generator 8-2, 8-5, 8-10	Practice 7-6, 7-7, 8-6 Reteaching 7-6, 7-7, 8-6 Enrichment 7-6, 7-7, 8-6 Computer Test Generator 7-6, 7-7, 8-6	Practice 10-1, 10-2, 10-3, 10-7 Reteaching 10-1, 10-2, 10-3, 10-7 Enrichment 10-1, 10-2, 10-3, 10-7 Computer Test Generator 10-1, 10-2, 10-3, 10-7
Integer Awareness	29–32			Practice 11-1, 11-2 Reteaching 11-1, 11-2 Enrichment 11-1, 11-2 Computer Test Generator 11-1, 11-2	Practice 1-6 Reteaching 1-6 Enrichment 1-6 Computer Test Generator 1-6	Practice 1-2 Reteaching 1-2 Enrichment 1-2 Computer Test Generator 1-2	Practice 1-4 Reteaching 1-4 Enrichment 1-4 Computer Test Generator 1-4

Parent's or Guardian's signature _____

Student Progress Chart—Basic Skills Test (continued)

Skill	Test Items	Number of Items Correct	Demonstrates Skill? (yes or no)	Suggested Remediation*†			
				Prentice Hall Mathematics Course 1	Prentice Hall Mathematics Course 2	Prentice Hall Mathematics Course 3	Prentice Hall Mathematics Pre-Algebra
Integer Operations	33–36			Practice 11-3, 11-4, 11-5, 11-6, 11-7 Reteaching 11-3, 11-4, 11-5, 11-6, 11-7 Enrichment 11-3, 11-4, 11-5, 11-6, 11-7 Computer Test Generator 11-3, 11-4, 11-5, 11-6, 11-7	Practice 1-7, 1-8 Reteaching 1-7, 1-8 Enrichment 1-7, 1-8 Computer Test Generator 1-7, 1-8	Practice 1-3, 1-4 Reteaching 1-3, 1-4 Enrichment 1-3, 1-4 Computer Test Generator 1-3, 1-4	Practice 1-5, 1-6, 1-9 Reteaching 1-5, 1-6, 1-9 Enrichment 1-5, 1-6, 1-9 Computer Test Generator 1-5, 1-6, 1-9
Translating Words into Mathematical Expressions	37–40			Practice 3-2, 3-3 Reteaching 3-2, 3-3 Enrichment 3-2, 3-3 Computer Test Generator 3-2, 3-3	Practice 4-1 Reteaching 4-1 Enrichment 4-1 Computer Test Generator 4-1	Practice 1-1 Reteaching 1-1 Enrichment 1-1 Computer Test Generator 1-1	Practice 1-1 Reteaching 1-1 Enrichment 1-1 Computer Test Generator 1-1
Solving One-Step Equations	41–44			Practice 3-5, 3-6, 3-7 Reteaching 3-5, 3-6, 3-7 Enrichment 3-5, 3-6, 3-7 Computer Test Generator 3-5, 3-6, 3-7	Practice 4-3, 4-4 Reteaching 4-3, 4-4 Enrichment 4-3, 4-4 Computer Test Generator 4-3, 4-4	Practice 1-6, 1-7 Reteaching 1-6, 1-7 Enrichment 1-6, 1-7 Computer Test Generator 1-6, 1-7	Practice 2-5, 2-6 Reteaching 2-5, 2-6 Enrichment 2-5, 2-6 Computer Test Generator 2-5, 2-6

Name _____ Class _____ Date _____

End-of-Year Student Progress Chart

Basic Skills Test

Skill	Test Items	Number of Items Correct	Demonstrates Skill? (yes or no)
Decimal Operations	1–4		
Factors and Prime Numbers	5–8		
Fraction Operations	9–12		
Exponent Awareness	13–16		
Proportional Reasoning	17–20		
Percents	21–24		
Finding Perimeter, Area, and Volume	25–28		
Integer Awareness	29–32		
Integer Operations	33–36		
Translating Words into Mathematical Expressions	37–40		
Solving One-Step Equations	41–44		

Algebra Concept-Readiness Test

Concept	Test Items	Number of Items Correct	Demonstrates Skill? (yes or no)
The Distributive Property	1–6		
Square Roots	7–12		
Writing Equations	13–18		
Solving Equations Using the Properties of Equality	19–24		
Graphing	25–30		

Teacher's Comments

_____

_____

_____

Recommended Next Course _____

_____   _____
Teacher's Signature   **Parent's or Guardian's Signature**

Algebra Readiness Tests–Student Progress Chart for Basic Skills Test

Dear Family,

Algebra is an important course in a student's education. We want to prepare students now so they have the skills they'll need to succeed in Algebra.

To help gauge students' readiness for Algebra, our Prentice Hall Mathematics program provides "Algebra Readiness Tests." Students take these tests at the beginning of, during, or at the end of the school year.

There are two types of Algebra Readiness Tests—a Basic Skills Test and an Algebra Concept-Readiness Test.

Your child recently took a Basic Skills Test. The Student Progress Chart accompanying this letter shows the results, including:

- the number of questions your child answered correctly for each basic skill
- whether your child has demonstrated the skill in question
- review material your child can use to practice skills

Of course, these tests are not the only tools we use to evaluate Algebra readiness. Other factors are also important, such as: performance in other tests during the school year; homework and other assessment tools, such as projects and journals; standardized tests; school attendance and attitude; organizational skills; and study habits.

Please review the Student Progress Chart with your child. There is a space for your signature, to indicate that you've reviewed the chart. Please sign the chart and return it to me.

Sincerely,

_____

Algebra Readiness Tests–
End-of-Year Student Progress Chart

Dear Family,

With the end of the school year approaching, now is a good time to review students' readiness for future Math courses, including Algebra.

To help gauge students' readiness for Algebra, our Prentice Hall Mathematics program provides "Algebra Readiness Tests," comprising a Basic Skills Test and an Algebra Concept-Readiness Test.

The End-of-Year Student Progress Chart accompanying this letter shows the test results for your child, including:

- the number of questions your child answered correctly for each skill
- whether your child has demonstrated the skill in question
- teacher's comments and recommendations for your child's next course

Of course, these tests are not the only tools we use to evaluate Algebra readiness. Other factors are also important, such as: performance in other tests during the school year; homework and other assessment tools, such as projects and journals; standardized tests; school attendance and attitude; organizational skills; and study habits.

Please review the End-of-Year Student Progress Chart with your child. There is a space for your signature, to indicate that you've reviewed the chart. Please sign the chart and return it to me.

Sincerely,

_____

Answers to Test Excercises

Basic Skills Test, Form A

1. B 2. C 3. A 4. A
5. B 6. D 7. A 8. B
9. C 10. D 11. D 12. A
13. C 14. C 15. B 16. A
17. D 18. A 19. D 20. C
21. C 22. D 23. B 24. A
25. A 26. C 27. D 28. A
29. A 30. B 31. C 32. D
33. B 34. C 35. A 36. D
37. D 38. B 39. C 40. C
41. A 42. B 43. D 44. B

Basic Skills Test, Form B

1. B 2. D 3. A 4. C
5. B 6. C 7. D 8. A
9. C 10. D 11. A 12. C
13. B 14. B 15. A 16. C
17. C 18. B 19. A 20. C
21. A 22. B 23. A 24. D
25. C 26. A 27. B 28. D
29. D 30. A 31. A 32. B
33. C 34. D 35. A 36. B
37. A 38. D 39. B 40. C
41. C 42. D 43. B 44. C

Basic Skills Test, Form C

1. D 2. A 3. A 4. B
5. C 6. B 7. C 8. B
9. D 10. B 11. C 12. A
13. B 14. A 15. D 16. B
17. B 18. C 19. B 20. D
21. A 22. C 23. B 24. D
25. D 26. B 27. A 28. B
29. C 30. A 31. B 32. D
33. A 34. C 35. D 36. B
37. C 38. A 39. B 40. C
41. D 42. A 43. C 44. D

Basic Skills Test, Form D

1. A 2. C 3. D 4. A
5. B 6. C 7. B 8. D
9. A 10. C 11. D 12. C
13. A 14. C 15. B 16. D
17. B 18. D 19. C 20. A
21. C 22. A 23. D 24. B
25. C 26. D 27. B 28. A
29. B 30. D 31. C 32. A
33. B 34. D 35. B 36. A
37. B 38. C 39. A 40. B
41. B 42. C 43. A 44. B

Algebra Concept-Readiness Test, Form A

1. C 2. C 3. C 4. D
5. A 6. D 7. A 8. B
9. C 10. A 11. D 12. B
13. C 14. A 15. C 16. D
17. B 18. D 19. D 20. A
21. B 22. C 23. B 24. A
25. B 26. A 27. D 28. D
29. A 30. C

Algebra Concept-Readiness Test, Form B

1. C 2. A 3. C 4. B
5. D 6. A 7. C 8. B
9. A 10. D 11. C 12. C
13. B 14. D 15. A 16. C
17. D 18. A 19. A 20. B
21. C 22. D 23. C 24. B
25. C 26. B 27. C 28. D
29. A 30. B